Dare to Dream,

Believe to Achieve Conquering Doubt on the Path to Success

Farha

The first edition was published in 2023

ISBN:
Published by:
Sunshine
1663 Liberty Drive
Hyderabad, IN 47403
www.Sunshinepublishers.com

This book is self-published using on-demand printing and publishing, which allows it to be printed and distributed globally

TABLE OF CONTENTS

Chapter 1: The Power of Belief

The Role of Belief in Achieving Goals

In the journey towards success, belief plays a crucial role. Doubt can often creep into our minds, casting shadows of uncertainty and hindering our progress. However, it is our unwavering belief that acts as a powerful guiding force, propelling us towards our goals. This subchapter will explore the significance of belief in achieving our dreams and provide practical strategies to overcome doubt.

Belief is the foundation upon which dreams are built. Without it, our aspirations remain stagnant, mere figments of our imagination. It is the belief that transforms these dreams into tangible goals, fuelling our determination to overcome obstacles and make them a reality. When we wholeheartedly believe in our capabilities and the possibility of success, we unleash a powerful energy that propels us forward, even in the face of adversity.

Doubt, on the other hand, is the enemy of progress. It whispers in our ears, sowing seeds of uncertainty and questioning our abilities. It is vital to recognize and confront these doubts head-on. By acknowledging their existence, we can begin to challenge them and replace them with positive affirmations. Surrounding ourselves with a supportive network of individuals who believe in us and our abilities can also help to counteract doubt.

To cultivate belief, it is essential to visualize our goals. By vividly imagining ourselves achieving what we desire, we create a sense of possibility and inevitability. This visualization technique harnesses the power of our subconscious mind, aligning our thoughts and actions towards our goals. Additionally, setting smaller milestones along the way provides tangible evidence of progress, further reinforcing our belief in our ability to achieve.

Another crucial component of belief is self-compassion. It is natural to face setbacks and encounter failures on our journey. Instead of allowing these moments to erode our belief, we must practice self-compassion and view them as opportunities for growth. By reframing failure as a stepping stone towards success, we can maintain our belief in the face of setbacks.

In conclusion, belief is an indispensable force in achieving our goals. It acts as the driving force that propels us towards success, despite doubt and uncertainty. By nurturing belief through visualization, setting milestones, and practicing self-compassion, we can conquer doubt and realize our dreams. So, dare to dream, believe in yourself, and embark on the path to success with unwavering conviction.

Understanding the Impact of Doubt

Doubt is a powerful emotion that can have a profound impact on our lives. It creeps into our minds, whispering negative thoughts and planting seeds of uncertainty. Whether it's self-doubt, doubt in others, or doubt about the future, it can hinder our progress and prevent us from reaching our full potential. In this subchapter, we will explore the various ways that doubt can impact our lives and provide strategies to overcome it on the path to success.

First and foremost, doubt can paralyze us, preventing us from taking action and pursuing our dreams. It acts as a barrier, keeping us trapped in our comfort zones and preventing us from taking risks. We become so consumed by our doubts that we fail to see the possibilities and opportunities that lie ahead. By understanding the impact of doubt, we can begin to break free from its grip and start making progress towards our goals.

Another way doubt impacts us is by eroding our self-confidence. When we doubt our abilities, we undermine our own potential for success. We become hesitant, second-guessing our decisions and questioning our every move. This lack of confidence can hinder our relationships, career growth, and overall happiness. By recognizing the detrimental effects of doubt, we can start building our self-esteem and belief in ourselves.

Doubt also affects our mindset and attitude. It breeds negativity and pessimism, making it difficult to see the silver lining in any situation. We become trapped in a cycle of self-doubt and negative thinking, which can lead to feelings of anxiety and depression. However, by understanding the impact of doubt, we can shift our mindset and cultivate a positive outlook on life.

To stop doubting and start living a more fulfilling life, it's essential to develop strategies to overcome doubt. These strategies include self-reflection, challenging negative thoughts, seeking support from others, and taking small steps towards our goals. By practicing self-awareness and acknowledging our doubts, we can gradually diminish their power over us.

In conclusion, doubt can have a significant impact on our lives. It can paralyze us, erode our self-confidence, and breed negativity. However, by understanding the impact of doubt and implementing strategies to overcome it, we can break free from its grip and pursue our dreams with confidence. Let go of doubt, embrace your true potential, and dare to dream.

Overcoming Self-Limiting Beliefs

In our journey towards success, one of the biggest obstacles we often encounter is our own self-limiting beliefs. These are the negative thoughts and doubts that hold us back from reaching our true potential. They stem from our past experiences, societal conditioning, and the fear of failure. However, it is essential to recognize that these beliefs are not based on reality but are merely illusions that we have created in our minds.

To stop doubting ourselves and break free from these self-imposed limitations, we must first understand the power of our thoughts. Our thoughts shape our reality, and if we continue to believe in our limitations, we will never be able to achieve our dreams. We must challenge these beliefs and replace them with empowering thoughts that align with our aspirations.

One effective way to overcome self-limiting beliefs is through self-reflection and awareness. Take a moment to observe your thoughts and identify the negative patterns that hold you back. Notice the moments when doubt creeps in and replace those thoughts with positive affirmations. Remind yourself of your strengths, accomplishments, and the potential within you.

Another crucial step in overcoming self-limiting beliefs is surrounding yourself with positive influences. Seek out mentors, friends, or like-minded individuals who uplift and inspire you. Their unwavering belief in your abilities will help you see beyond your self-imposed limitations. Additionally, engage in activities that push you outside of your comfort zone. By taking risks and facing challenges head-on, you will gradually build resilience and confidence.

Furthermore, it is imperative to celebrate small victories along the way. Acknowledge and appreciate your progress, no matter how insignificant it may seem. Each step forward is a testament to your ability to overcome self-doubt and conquer your limitations. By celebrating these achievements, you reinforce positive beliefs and build momentum towards greater success.

Remember, overcoming self-limiting beliefs is a continuous process. It requires patience, perseverance, and a commitment to personal growth. As you embark on this transformative journey, embrace the discomfort and challenges that come your way. Believe in your potential, dare to dream big, and trust that you have the power to achieve anything you set your mind to.

In conclusion, breaking free from self-limiting beliefs is essential to stop doubting ourselves and unlock our true potential. By cultivating self-awareness, surrounding ourselves with positive influences, celebrating small victories, and persisting through challenges, we can overcome these limitations and pave the path towards success. Dare to dream, believe in yourself, and watch as your doubts fade away, replaced by a newfound confidence that propels you towards greatness.

Chapter 2: Identifying and Challenging Doubt

Acknowledging Your Doubts

In our journey towards success, doubt often becomes an unwelcome companion. It creeps into our minds, whispering discouraging thoughts and planting seeds of uncertainty. Acknowledging your doubts is the first step towards conquering them and paving the way for a fulfilling and successful life.

Doubt is a natural human emotion that affects everyone at some point in their lives. It is important to remember that you are not alone in experiencing doubt. Even the most accomplished individuals have faced moments of uncertainty. The key lies in acknowledging your doubts and understanding that they do not define you or your potential for success.

One way to acknowledge your doubts is to confront them head-on. Take a moment to sit with your doubts, identify them, and understand where they stem from. Are they rooted in fear of failure, lack of self-confidence, or external influences? By understanding the source of your doubts, you can begin to address them effectively.

Another powerful approach is to practice self-reflection. Reflect on your past successes and the obstacles you have overcome. Remember that doubt is often a result of underestimating your abilities. By acknowledging your past achievements, you can build a strong foundation of self-belief and remind yourself that you are capable of achieving greatness.

It is essential to surround yourself with a support system that believes in you. Seek out individuals who uplift and encourage you, who can provide guidance and reassurance when doubt creeps in. Having a network of like-minded individuals can significantly impact your ability to overcome doubt and achieve your goals.

Furthermore, embracing a growth mindset is crucial in conquering doubt. Understand that every challenge and setback is an opportunity for growth and learning. Instead of viewing doubt as a roadblock, see it as a stepping stone towards personal and professional development. Embrace the discomfort and use it as fuel to push yourself further.

Remember, doubt is not a sign of weakness but an invitation to push beyond your comfort zone. By acknowledging your doubts and understanding their origins, you can take control of your journey towards success. Surround yourself with positivity, practice self-reflection, and embrace a growth mindset. Dare to dream, believe in yourself, and you will conquer doubt on the path to achieving greatness.

So, stop doubting and start believing in yourself. The journey towards success begins with acknowledging your doubts and taking the first step towards overcoming them. You have the power to conquer doubt and achieve your dreams. Dare to dream, believe to achieve!

Unmasking the Root Causes of Doubt

Doubt is a common emotion that plagues individuals of all walks of life. It arises when we question our abilities, decisions, or even our dreams. This subchapter aims to delve into the depths of doubt and uncover the root causes that often hold us back from achieving our true potential. By understanding these underlying factors, we can begin to address and overcome doubt with confidence and clarity.

One of the primary causes of doubt is fear. Fear can manifest itself in various forms, such as the fear of failure, the fear of judgment, or the fear of stepping out of our comfort zones. These fears often stem from past experiences or societal expectations, leading us to doubt our own capabilities. By acknowledging and confronting our fears head-on, we can start to dismantle doubts and build a foundation of self-belief.

Another significant cause of doubt is a lack of self-esteem. When we don't value ourselves or our abilities, doubt easily creeps in. Negative self-talk and comparison to others can erode our confidence, leaving us questioning our worthiness. To combat this, it is crucial to cultivate self-love and practice self-compassion. Recognizing our unique strengths and achievements can help bolster our self-esteem and diminish doubt in our abilities.

Additionally, external influences can play a role in fostering doubt. Negative people or unsupportive environments can fuel our insecurities and make us question our dreams. Surrounding ourselves with positive and encouraging individuals who believe in our potential can make a world of difference in conquering doubt. Seeking out mentors or joining supportive communities can provide the necessary encouragement to stay focused on our goals.

Moreover, past failures or setbacks can often contribute to doubt. When we've experienced disappointment or setbacks in the past, we may find it challenging to believe in our ability to succeed. However, it is crucial to reframe these failures as learning experiences and stepping stones towards growth. Embracing a growth mindset allows us to view setbacks as opportunities for improvement and propels us forward on the path to success.

In conclusion, doubt is a barrier that holds many individuals back from realizing their dreams and achieving their goals. By unmasking the root causes of doubt, such as fear, lack of self-esteem, external influences, and past failures, we can begin to dismantle its power over us. Through self-reflection, self-compassion, and surrounding ourselves with positive influences, we can build the necessary resilience and belief in ourselves to stop doubting and start pursuing our dreams with unwavering confidence.

Techniques for Challenging and Overcoming Doubt

Introduction:

Doubt is a common emotion that can hold us back from achieving our full potential. It can cloud our judgment, undermine our confidence, and prevent us from taking the necessary steps towards success. However, by developing effective techniques to challenge and overcome doubt, we can break free from its grip and move closer towards our dreams. In this subchapter, we will explore some powerful strategies to help you stop doubting and start believing in yourself.

1.   Identify   the   source   of   doubt:
The first step in overcoming doubt is to identify its source. Is it coming from external factors such as criticism or negative influences? Or is it originating internally from self-limiting beliefs? Understanding the root cause of doubt will empower you to address it more effectively.

2.   Reframe   negative   thoughts:
Challenge your negative thoughts and replace them with positive affirmations. Instead of focusing on what could go wrong, redirect your attention to what could go right. Train your mind to see obstacles as opportunities for growth and learning.

3.   Surround   yourself   with   positivity:
Surrounding yourself with supportive and positive individuals can make a significant impact on your ability to overcome doubt. Seek out like-minded people who believe in your abilities and aspirations. Their encouragement and belief in you will serve as a powerful antidote to doubt.

4.   Set   realistic   goals:
Setting realistic goals helps to build confidence and combat doubt. Break down your larger goals into smaller, achievable milestones. Each small victory will reinforce your belief in your abilities and propel you forward.

5.   Celebrate   past   successes:
Reflect on your past successes and remind yourself of the obstacles you have already overcome. Recall the times when you

defied doubt and achieved something remarkable. Use these memories as a source of inspiration and motivation during challenging times.

6. Embrace failure as a learning opportunity: Instead of letting failure fuel doubt, view it as a valuable learning opportunity. Understand that setbacks are a natural part of the journey towards success. Analyze what went wrong, learn from it, and make adjustments. Embracing failure as a stepping stone will help you grow stronger and more resilient.

Conclusion:
Doubt can be a formidable barrier on the path to success. However, by implementing these techniques, you can challenge and overcome doubt, allowing yourself to dare to dream and believe in your ability to achieve. Remember, self-belief is a powerful tool that can transform your life. Trust in yourself and your capabilities, and watch as doubt becomes a thing of the past.

Chapter 3: Setting Meaningful and Attainable Goals

The Importance of Goal Setting

In the journey towards success, one vital element often overlooked is the power of goal setting. Setting clear, achievable goals can provide the necessary direction and motivation to overcome doubt and achieve greatness. Whether you are an aspiring entrepreneur, a student, or simply someone striving for personal growth, understanding the importance of goal setting is essential to stop doubting yourself and start achieving your dreams.

Goals serve as a roadmap, guiding individuals to their desired destination. Without a clear direction, doubt can creep in, leading to indecision and lack of progress. When you set specific goals, you are essentially creating a blueprint for success. These goals act as a compass, keeping you focused and driven, even in the face of uncertainty. Each milestone reached brings a sense of accomplishment, gradually eroding doubt and replacing it with confidence.

Furthermore, goal setting provides a sense of purpose and meaning. When you have a vision for what you want to achieve, you are more likely to find fulfillment and satisfaction in your endeavors. Without goals, doubt can easily seep into your thoughts, making you question the value and purpose of your actions. By setting ambitious yet attainable goals, you create a sense of purpose that ignites your passion and fuels your determination to succeed.

Setting goals also helps in breaking down overwhelming tasks into manageable steps. Doubt often arises when faced with seemingly insurmountable challenges. However, by breaking down your goals into smaller, actionable tasks, doubt is replaced with a sense of progress and accomplishment. Each small step taken brings you closer to your ultimate goal, reinforcing your belief in your abilities and diminishing doubt along the way.

Moreover, goal setting cultivates a growth mindset. It encourages you to continuously strive for improvement and pushes you out of your comfort zone. By setting goals that challenge you, doubt is transformed into an opportunity for growth and self-discovery. Each setback becomes a learning experience, propelling you further along the path to success.

In conclusion, goal setting is the cornerstone of conquering doubt and achieving success. By setting clear, achievable goals, you provide yourself with direction, purpose, and motivation. It enables you to break down overwhelming tasks, cultivates a growth mindset, and brings a sense of fulfillment and accomplishment. So, dare to dream, believe in yourself, and set goals that will propel you towards the life you desire.

Creating SMART Goals

Setting goals is a crucial step towards achieving success in any aspect of life. Whether you are trying to overcome self-doubt or achieve your dreams, having specific, measurable, attainable, relevant, and time-bound (SMART) goals can provide you with a roadmap to success. In this subchapter, we will explore the process of creating SMART goals and how they can help you conquer doubt on your path to success.

Specificity is the key to effective goal setting. When setting your goals, be clear and specific about what you want to achieve. Instead of saying, "I want to overcome self-doubt," specify the area you want to work on, such as public speaking or pursuing a new career. By being specific, you can focus your efforts and measure your progress more effectively.

Measurability allows you to track your progress and stay motivated along the way. Break down your goals into measurable components. For example, if your goal is to improve your public speaking skills, you can measure your progress by tracking the number of presentations you do or the level of confidence you feel during each one. Measuring your progress will help you stay accountable and give you a sense of accomplishment as you achieve milestones.

Attainability ensures that your goals are realistic and achievable. While it is important to dream big, setting unrealistic goals can lead to disappointment and self-doubt. Assess your skills, resources, and time constraints to set attainable goals that challenge you without overwhelming you. Remember, small steps towards your goals are better than no steps at all.

Relevance ensures that your goals align with your values, passions, and overall vision. Ask yourself why you want to achieve a particular goal. Is it something that truly matters to you, or are you pursuing it to please others? Setting goals that are meaningful to you will provide the necessary motivation to overcome doubt and persevere through challenges.

Time-bound goals have a deadline, which creates a sense of urgency and prevents procrastination. Set deadlines for each step of your goal and hold yourself accountable. Breaking your goals into smaller, time-bound tasks will make them more manageable and increase your chances of success.

In conclusion, creating SMART goals is an essential tool in conquering doubt on your path to success. By setting specific, measurable, attainable, relevant, and time-bound goals, you can stay focused, motivated, and track your progress effectively. Remember to dream big, believe in yourself, and take small steps towards your goals. With a clear roadmap in place, you can overcome self-doubt and achieve the success you desire.

Aligning Goals with Personal Values and Passions

In the journey towards success, it is crucial to align our goals with our personal values and passions. This subchapter aims to guide you on this transformative path, helping you conquer doubt and forge ahead with unwavering determination. Whether you are a student, an aspiring entrepreneur, or a professional seeking career advancement, the principles outlined here will resonate with anyone looking to stop doubting and start achieving.

At the core of this chapter lies the concept of self-reflection. It is essential to take a step back and evaluate what truly matters to you. What are your core values? What are the passions that ignite your soul? Understanding these aspects of yourself will enable you to set meaningful goals that align with who you are as a person. When your goals are rooted in your values and passions, you will find the motivation and drive to pursue them relentlessly.

To align your goals with your personal values, it is necessary to identify what is truly important to you. Is it making a positive impact on your community? Is it cultivating meaningful relationships? Or is it achieving financial security? Once you have identified your values, you can then set goals that reflect and support these values. For example, if making a positive impact is a core value, you may set a goal to volunteer regularly or start a non-profit organization.

Similarly, aligning your goals with your passions adds an extra layer of fulfillment to your journey. When you are passionate about something, it becomes easier to overcome obstacles and stay committed. Identify what excites you, what makes you feel alive, and incorporate those passions into your goals. For instance, if you are passionate about writing, you may set a goal to publish a book or start a blog.

Remember, aligning goals with personal values and passions is not a one-time exercise. It requires continuous self-reflection and adjustment. As you grow and evolve, your values and passions may change, and so may your goals. Embrace this evolution, and be open to realigning your goals accordingly.

By aligning your goals with your personal values and passions, you will find yourself on a path filled with purpose and fulfillment. Doubt will dissipate, and you will be empowered to take bold steps towards success. Dare to dream, believe in yourself, and let your values and passions guide you to the extraordinary life you deserve.

Chapter 4: Developing a Positive Mindset

Cultivating a Growth Mindset

In the journey towards success, one of the most crucial aspects is developing a growth mindset. This subchapter aims to guide and inspire you to cultivate a growth mindset, enabling you to conquer doubt and achieve your dreams. Whether you are a student, professional, entrepreneur, or anyone striving for success, this chapter is dedicated to helping you stop doubting and start believing in your abilities.

A growth mindset is the belief that your abilities and intelligence can be developed through dedication, hard work, and perseverance. It is the understanding that failure is not a permanent setback but an opportunity for growth and learning. With a growth mindset, you embrace challenges, persist in the face of obstacles, and view criticism as constructive feedback.

The first step towards cultivating a growth mindset is to develop self-awareness. Take a moment to reflect on your current beliefs and attitudes towards success and failure. Are you often overwhelmed by doubt and fear of failure? Do you view setbacks as proof of your limitations? Recognizing these negative thought patterns is essential to break free from their grip.

Next, start reframing your mindset by embracing challenges. Rather than avoiding difficult tasks, actively seek them out. Remember, every challenge is an opportunity to learn something new and improve your skills. Embrace setbacks as valuable lessons and use them to adjust your strategies and approach towards your goals.

To foster a growth mindset, surround yourself with positive influences. Seek out mentors, coaches, or like-minded individuals who can support and encourage your growth. Engage in personal development activities such as reading inspirational books, attending workshops, or joining communities of individuals with similar aspirations.

Furthermore, practice self-compassion and celebrate small wins along the way. Acknowledge your progress and give yourself credit for your efforts. This will boost your confidence and motivate you to continue pushing forward.

Remember, cultivating a growth mindset is a lifelong journey. Embrace the process and be patient with yourself. Success does not happen overnight, but with dedication, perseverance, and a growth mindset, you have the power to conquer doubt and achieve your dreams.

In conclusion, developing a growth mindset is vital for overcoming doubt and achieving success. By embracing challenges, reframing setbacks, seeking support, and practicing self-compassion, you can cultivate a mindset that thrives on growth and learning. So, dare to dream, believe in your abilities, and embark on the path to success with a renewed sense of confidence and determination.

Practicing Self-Compassion

In our journey towards success, self-compassion is an essential tool that often gets overlooked. We are so focused on achieving our goals and conquering doubt that we forget to be kind and forgiving towards ourselves. However, by incorporating self-compassion into our daily lives, we can effectively stop doubting and pave the way for a more fulfilling and successful future.

Self-compassion refers to treating ourselves with the same kindness and understanding that we would offer to a loved one. It involves recognizing our imperfections, mistakes, and setbacks without judgment or self-criticism. Practicing self-compassion helps us build resilience, boost self-esteem, and cultivate a positive mindset.

One of the first steps towards self-compassion is acknowledging that it is okay to make mistakes. We are all human beings, and mistakes are a natural part of our growth and learning process. Instead of berating ourselves for our failures, we can choose to view them as valuable lessons and opportunities for growth. By embracing our imperfections, we allow ourselves to move forward with renewed determination and a sense of self-acceptance.

Another aspect of self-compassion is giving ourselves permission to take care of our physical, emotional, and mental well-being. Often, we become so consumed with our goals that we neglect our own needs. We push ourselves to the brink of exhaustion, thinking that it is the only way to achieve success. However, by practicing self-compassion, we learn to prioritize self-care and set healthy boundaries. This allows us to recharge, refocus, and approach our goals with a renewed sense of energy and clarity.

Additionally, practicing self-compassion involves cultivating a positive inner dialogue. We tend to be our own harshest critics, constantly doubting our abilities and questioning our worth. By consciously replacing negative self-talk with positive affirmations and kind words, we can shift our mindset towards a more empowering and self-assured state. We can start to believe in ourselves, our dreams, and our ability to overcome doubt.

In conclusion, incorporating self-compassion into our lives is crucial for conquering doubt and achieving success. By embracing our mistakes, prioritizing self-care, and fostering a positive inner dialogue, we can build resilience, boost self-esteem, and cultivate a mindset of unwavering belief in ourselves. So, dare to practice self-compassion and believe in your ability to achieve greatness.

Harnessing the Power of Positive Affirmations

In our journey towards success, doubt often becomes a formidable obstacle that holds us back. It infiltrates our thoughts, weakens our resolve, and prevents us from reaching our full potential. However, there is a powerful tool that can help us conquer doubt and propel us towards achieving our dreams: positive affirmations.

Positive affirmations are statements that we repeat to ourselves, designed to challenge negative thoughts and replace them with empowering beliefs. When we harness the power of positive affirmations, we can transform our mindset and create a foundation for success.

The first step in utilizing positive affirmations is to identify the doubts and negative beliefs that are hindering our progress. These doubts may include thoughts such as "I'm not good enough," "I'll never succeed," or "I don't have what it takes." Once we have identified these limiting beliefs, we can counteract them with positive affirmations that challenge and replace them.

For example, if we find ourselves doubting our abilities, we can affirm, "I am capable and skilled in achieving my goals." By repeating this affirmation regularly, we begin to rewire our subconscious mind, replacing self-doubt with confidence and self-assurance.

The key to effective positive affirmations lies in their repetition and consistency. By consistently repeating affirmations, we reinforce positive beliefs and gradually weaken the power of doubt. It is essential to integrate affirmations into our daily routine, perhaps through morning or evening rituals, to ensure they become ingrained in our subconscious.

Moreover, it is crucial to make our affirmations as specific, vivid, and emotionally charged as possible. Instead of simply stating, "I am successful," we can expand it to, "I am wildly successful in my chosen career, making a positive impact while experiencing joy and abundance." The more detailed and emotionally resonant our affirmations are, the more effective they become in reprogramming our minds.

Harnessing the power of positive affirmations can have a profound impact on all aspects of our lives. As we replace doubt with belief and negativity with positivity, we open ourselves up to new opportunities, attract success, and cultivate a resilient mindset.

So, dare to dream and believe in your abilities. Embrace positive affirmations as your secret weapon to stop doubting and start achieving. With consistency, repetition, and a commitment to challenging negative thoughts, you can conquer doubt on your path to success. Remember, you have the power within you to achieve greatness, and positive affirmations will guide you every step of the way.

Chapter 5: Building Resilience in the Face of Setbacks

Understanding the Nature of Setbacks

In our journey towards success, setbacks are inevitable. They are an integral part of life and play a crucial role in shaping our character and resilience. Recognizing and understanding the nature of setbacks is essential if we are to conquer doubt and achieve our dreams. In this subchapter, we will delve into the various aspects of setbacks and discover how to navigate through them with strength and determination.

Setbacks come in different forms and sizes. They can be a failed business venture, a rejection letter, a lost opportunity, or even a personal setback like a health issue. Regardless of their nature, setbacks often lead to doubt and can make us question our abilities and aspirations. However, it is important to remember that setbacks are not indications of failure; rather, they are stepping stones towards growth and success.

One key aspect of setbacks is that they provide valuable learning experiences. Each setback presents an opportunity to reflect on our approach, identify areas for improvement, and develop new strategies. Embracing setbacks as lessons rather than failures allows us to gain wisdom, refine our skills, and strengthen our resolve to overcome future challenges.

Another crucial aspect of setbacks is resilience. How we respond to setbacks defines our character and determines our ability to bounce back. It is important to cultivate a mindset that perceives setbacks as temporary obstacles rather than insurmountable roadblocks. By maintaining a positive attitude, seeking support from others, and focusing on our long-term goals, we can build the resilience necessary to overcome setbacks and continue moving forward.

Moreover, setbacks often provide an opportunity for self-reflection and introspection. They allow us to reassess our values, priorities, and motivations. By understanding our true desires and aligning them with our actions, setbacks can serve as catalysts for personal growth and self-discovery.

To truly conquer doubt and achieve our dreams, it is essential to understand that setbacks are not the end of the road but rather detours on our journey. By recognizing setbacks as valuable learning experiences, cultivating resilience, and embracing self-reflection, we can transform setbacks into opportunities for growth and success.

In conclusion, setbacks are an inevitable part of life, but they do not define our ultimate success or failure. By understanding their nature, we can navigate through setbacks with confidence, learn from them, and use them as stepping stones towards achieving our dreams. So, let us embrace setbacks, conquer doubt, and dare to dream, believe to achieve.

Embracing Failure as a Learning Opportunity

Failure is often viewed as a setback, a sign of defeat or inadequacy. However, in the journey towards success, failure can be one of the most valuable and transformative experiences. In this subchapter, we will explore the concept of embracing failure as a learning opportunity and how it can help us conquer doubt on the path to success.

Many successful individuals have attributed their achievements to their ability to learn from failures. Thomas Edison, the inventor of the light bulb, famously said, "I have not failed. I've just found 10,000 ways that won't work." This mindset shift is crucial in overcoming doubt and embracing failure as a stepping stone to success.

When we view failure as an opportunity to learn and grow, it becomes a catalyst for personal development. Each failure provides valuable insights, teaches us important lessons, and helps us discover our strengths and weaknesses. By analyzing what went wrong, we gain a deeper understanding of our own abilities and areas that require improvement.

Embracing failure also helps us develop resilience. It teaches us to bounce back from setbacks and challenges, fostering a mindset that is essential for success. When we fear failure, doubt creeps in and holds us back from taking risks. However, by embracing failure, we become more willing to step out of our comfort zones, try new things, and pursue our dreams with confidence.

Moreover, failure provides an opportunity for innovation and creativity. It forces us to think outside the box, to find alternative approaches, and to adapt our strategies. Many groundbreaking inventions and discoveries have emerged from failed attempts, showcasing the power of failure as a catalyst for progress.

To embrace failure as a learning opportunity, it's important to change our perspective and mindset. Instead of dwelling on the negative aspects of failure, focus on the lessons learned and the growth experienced. Celebrate the courage it took to try, and acknowledge that failure is a natural part of the journey towards success.

In conclusion, embracing failure as a learning opportunity is a powerful mindset shift that can help us conquer doubt on the path to success. By viewing failure as a stepping stone rather than a defeat, we open ourselves up to valuable lessons, personal growth, resilience, and innovation. So, let us dare to dream, believe in ourselves, and embrace failure as a necessary and transformative part of our journey towards achieving our goals.

Strategies for Bouncing Back and Moving Forward

In life, setbacks and challenges are inevitable. We all face moments of doubt and uncertainty that can hinder our progress and make us question our abilities. However, it is important to remember that these moments do not define us. The key lies in developing effective strategies to bounce back and move forward, even in the face of adversity. In this subchapter, we will explore some powerful strategies that will help you conquer doubt and steer yourself towards success.

1. Embrace Failure as a Learning Opportunity: Instead of viewing failure as a roadblock, see it as a chance to learn and grow. Understand that setbacks are an integral part of the journey to success. Analyze what went wrong, learn from your mistakes, and use that knowledge to make better decisions in the future.

2. Cultivate a Positive Mindset: Train your mind to focus on the positive aspects of any situation. By shifting your perspective, you can find silver linings even in the most challenging times. Surround yourself with positive influences, practice gratitude, and engage in affirmations to rewire your thoughts and beliefs.

3. Set Achievable Goals: Break down your larger goals into smaller, more manageable tasks. This allows you to make progress step by step, boosting your confidence and motivation along the way. Celebrate each achievement, no matter how small, to stay motivated and keep moving forward.

4. Seek Support from Others: Surround yourself with individuals who uplift and support you. Share your goals and aspirations with trusted friends, family members, or mentors who can provide guidance and encouragement when doubt creeps in. Their belief in you can help you stay focused on your path to success.

5. Practice Self-Care: Take care of your physical, mental, and emotional well-being. Prioritize activities that replenish your energy and reduce stress, such as exercise, meditation, or spending time in nature. By taking care of yourself, you will be

better equipped to handle challenges and maintain a positive mindset.

6. Learn from Successful Individuals: Study the journeys of those who have achieved what you aspire to. Read books, listen to podcasts, or attend lectures by successful individuals in your field. Their stories of overcoming doubt and achieving greatness will inspire you and provide valuable insights.

Remember, doubt is a natural part of the human experience. It is what we do with that doubt that truly matters. By implementing these strategies for bouncing back and moving forward, you can conquer doubt and pave the way towards achieving your dreams. Embrace the challenges, believe in yourself, and never stop moving forward on your path to success.

Chapter 6: Surrounding Yourself with Supportive Influences

Recognizing the Importance of a Support System

In our journey towards success, it is easy to underestimate the power of having a strong support system. Often, we believe that we can achieve our goals on our own, relying solely on our own abilities and determination. However, recognizing the importance of a support system is crucial in conquering doubt and achieving our dreams.

Having a support system provides us with a network of individuals who believe in us, encourage us, and offer guidance when we face obstacles. Whether it is friends, family, mentors, or a community, these individuals play a vital role in helping us overcome self-doubt and push through challenging times.

One of the primary benefits of a support system is the emotional support they provide. When we doubt ourselves or face setbacks, having someone to lean on and share our concerns with can be incredibly reassuring. They can offer a fresh perspective, remind us of our strengths, and provide encouragement when we need it most. Their belief in us often fuels our own self-belief, helping us regain confidence in our abilities.

Moreover, a strong support system can offer practical support. They can provide advice, share their own experiences, and offer resources that can be instrumental in our journey towards success. They can introduce us to valuable connections, provide opportunities, or even act as an accountability partner, keeping us focused and motivated.

Additionally, a support system can serve as a source of inspiration. Surrounding ourselves with like-minded individuals who share similar goals and ambitions can be incredibly motivating. Witnessing their progress, success, and determination can ignite our own passion and belief in what we can achieve.

Lastly, a support system also helps us maintain a balanced perspective. They can provide honest feedback, offer constructive criticism, and challenge our limiting beliefs. They can help us identify our blind spots and push us to grow and improve.

Recognizing the importance of a support system is essential in conquering doubt and achieving success. To stop doubting ourselves, we need to surround ourselves with individuals who uplift and inspire us, who push us to overcome obstacles, and who remind us of our potential. By cultivating a strong support system, we create a foundation of belief and encouragement that can propel us towards our dreams.

Nurturing Relationships that Encourage and Inspire

In our quest to conquer doubt on the path to success, one crucial aspect often overlooked is the power of nurturing relationships. As human beings, we are social creatures, and the connections we form with others can have a profound impact on our mindset and accomplishments. By surrounding ourselves with individuals who encourage and inspire us, we create a supportive environment that fuels our determination and helps us overcome self-doubt.

Building strong relationships begins with being intentional about the people we choose to have in our lives. It is essential to surround ourselves with individuals who believe in our dreams and aspirations. These are the people who will provide the much-needed motivation and reassurance when self-doubt creeps in. They will remind us of our strengths, push us to pursue our goals, and offer constructive feedback when necessary.

Moreover, nurturing relationships that encourage and inspire involve reciprocity. It is not solely about receiving support but also about giving it. By being a source of inspiration for others, we create a positive cycle of encouragement. When we uplift and motivate those around us, we become part of a community that shares a common goal: to conquer doubt and achieve success. This interconnectedness strengthens our resolve and reminds us that we are not alone on this journey.

In nurturing relationships, it is crucial to foster open and honest communication. Being able to share our doubts and fears with trusted individuals creates a safe space where vulnerability is embraced. Through open dialogue, we can gain valuable insights and perspectives that may help us overcome our doubts. Additionally, these conversations can lead to collaborative problem-solving and the generation of innovative ideas.

To nurture relationships that encourage and inspire, we must also practice active listening. By truly hearing and understanding the experiences and perspectives of others, we can cultivate empathy and deepen our connection. This attentiveness allows us to provide meaningful support and encouragement tailored to the needs of our loved ones.

In conclusion, nurturing relationships that encourage and inspire is a vital component of conquering doubt on the path to success. Surrounding ourselves with individuals who believe in us, fostering reciprocity, and practicing open communication and active listening are all crucial steps in building these connections. By investing in these relationships, we create a network of support that can help us overcome self-doubt, stay motivated, and achieve our dreams. Remember, you are never alone on this journey – together, we can dare to dream and believe to achieve.

Seeking Mentorship and Guidance from Role Models

In our journey towards success, doubt often creeps in and clouds our judgment. We find ourselves questioning our abilities and second-guessing our dreams. However, there is a powerful tool that can help us conquer doubt and propel us towards our goals: seeking mentorship and guidance from role models.

Role models are individuals who have achieved what we aspire to accomplish. They serve as a beacon of inspiration, showing us that our dreams are indeed attainable. By connecting with role models, we expose ourselves to their wisdom, experience, and guidance, which can significantly impact our journey to success.

One of the key benefits of seeking mentorship is the opportunity to learn from someone who has navigated similar challenges. Role models have already encountered and overcome obstacles that we may face along our path. They can provide invaluable insights, advice, and strategies to help us overcome doubts and hurdles that may arise.

Mentors also offer a fresh perspective on our goals and aspirations. They can help us identify blind spots and areas for improvement, pushing us to grow beyond our limits. Their guidance can provide us with a roadmap to success, helping us navigate through unfamiliar territories with confidence.

Additionally, mentors can serve as a source of encouragement and motivation. They have been in our shoes and understand the doubts and fears we may be experiencing. Their support can provide us with the reassurance we need to stay focused and persevere, even during challenging times.

To find a mentor or role model, start by identifying individuals who have achieved what you aspire to accomplish. Look for people who share similar values and have demonstrated excellence in the areas that interest you. Reach out to them through networking events, social media platforms, or professional organizations.

When approaching a potential mentor, be respectful of their time and make it clear why you admire and value their expertise. Seek opportunities to learn from them, whether it be through regular meetings, attending their workshops, or shadowing them in their work. Remember, mentorship is a two-way street, so be willing to offer your time and support in return.

By seeking mentorship and guidance from role models, we can conquer doubt and realize our full potential. Their wisdom, experience, and support can ignite a fire within us, propelling us towards success. Remember, it's never too late to find a mentor and embark on a journey of growth and achievement. Dare to dream, believe to achieve!

Chapter 7: Taking Action Towards Your Dreams

Creating an Action Plan

In the journey towards achieving our dreams, doubt can often creep in and hinder our progress. It is vital to address this doubt head-on and develop an action plan that will help us conquer it and move forward. This subchapter aims to guide you through the process of creating an effective action plan that will enable you to stop doubting and start achieving your goals.

The first step in creating an action plan is to define your goal clearly. What is it that you want to achieve? Whether it's starting a new business, pursuing a passion, or improving a particular aspect of your life, being specific about your goal is essential. Write it down and visualize yourself already achieving it.

Next, break down your goal into smaller, manageable tasks. This will help you avoid feeling overwhelmed and make your goal seem more attainable. Identify the steps you need to take to reach your objective and set deadlines for each task. By setting deadlines, you create a sense of urgency and accountability.

Once you have your tasks and deadlines in place, it's time to prioritize. Determine which tasks are crucial for achieving your goal and focus on them first. Prioritization ensures that you allocate your time and energy efficiently, maximizing your chances of success.

As you work on your action plan, remember that doubt may still linger. Acknowledge it but don't let it paralyze you. Instead, challenge your doubts with positive affirmations and remind yourself of your capabilities and past achievements. Surround yourself with a support system of like-minded individuals who can provide encouragement and motivation when doubt tries to creep back in.

Regularly review and adjust your action plan as needed. Life is unpredictable, and circumstances may change. By regularly assessing your progress and making necessary adjustments, you ensure that your action plan remains relevant and effective.

In conclusion, creating an action plan is a crucial step in conquering doubt and achieving success. By defining your goal, breaking it down into manageable tasks, setting deadlines, prioritizing, challenging doubt, and reviewing your plan regularly, you will be well on your way to overcoming doubt and realizing your dreams. Remember, you have the power within you to stop doubting and start achieving. Dare to dream, believe in yourself, and take action today!

Overcoming Procrastination and Taking Initiative

Procrastination is a common obstacle that many individuals face on their journey towards success. It is the act of delaying or postponing tasks, often due to a lack of motivation, fear of failure, or feeling overwhelmed by the magnitude of the task at hand. However, to conquer doubt and achieve our dreams, it is crucial to overcome this tendency and take initiative.

One of the key strategies to overcome procrastination is to break tasks into smaller, manageable chunks. When we perceive a task as too daunting, it becomes easier to put it off. By breaking it down into smaller steps, we create a sense of progress and accomplishment, which motivates us to take action. This approach allows us to focus on one step at a time, gradually building momentum towards our goals.

Another effective technique is to create a schedule and set deadlines for ourselves. When we have a clear plan and specific timelines, it becomes easier to hold ourselves accountable and avoid the temptation to procrastinate. By committing to a set schedule, we prioritize our tasks and eliminate the option of postponing them indefinitely.

Moreover, it is essential to identify and address the underlying reasons behind our procrastination. Are we afraid of failure? Do we lack confidence in our abilities? By understanding the root causes, we can work on building self-belief and developing strategies to overcome these doubts. Seeking support from mentors, friends, or joining support groups can also provide valuable guidance and encouragement.

Taking initiative is closely tied to overcoming procrastination. It means stepping out of our comfort zones and taking action towards our goals, rather than waiting for opportunities to come our way. Initiative requires self-motivation, determination, and a willingness to take risks. By seizing opportunities when they arise and actively seeking new ones, we demonstrate our commitment to our dreams and increase our chances of success.

In conclusion, overcoming procrastination and taking initiative are vital steps towards conquering doubt and achieving our dreams. By breaking tasks into smaller steps, creating schedules, addressing underlying reasons for procrastination, and actively seizing opportunities, we can overcome doubt and move closer to success. Remember, it is never too late to start taking action – the journey of a thousand miles begins with a single step. So, dare to dream, believe in yourself, and take the initiative to turn those dreams into reality.

Maintaining Motivation and Momentum

In our journey toward success, doubt can often creep in and hinder our progress. It is natural to question our abilities and wonder if we have what it takes to achieve our dreams. However, it is important to remember that doubt is just an obstacle that can be overcome. In this subchapter, we will explore strategies for maintaining motivation and momentum, enabling us to push past doubt and move closer to our goals.

One of the most effective ways to maintain motivation is to set clear and achievable goals. By breaking down our dreams into smaller, manageable tasks, we can create a roadmap that guides us towards success. These goals should be challenging enough to keep us motivated, yet realistic enough to be attainable. As we accomplish each goal, we build momentum and gain confidence, fueling our motivation to keep going.

Another key factor in maintaining motivation is to surround ourselves with positive influences. Negative people and environments can drain our energy and fuel doubt. Instead, we should seek out individuals who inspire and support us. Joining communities or finding mentors who have already achieved what we aspire to can provide us with valuable guidance and encouragement along the way. Their success stories can serve as a reminder that our dreams are within reach.

To maintain momentum, it is crucial to celebrate our achievements, no matter how small they may seem. Recognizing our progress and giving ourselves credit for the hard work we have put in can boost our confidence and reinforce our motivation. Additionally, incorporating regular self-care practices, such as exercise, meditation, or hobbies, can help us recharge and stay focused on our goals.

When doubt creeps in, it is vital to reframe our mindset and focus on the positives. Rather than dwelling on what could go wrong, we should shift our attention to what we have already accomplished and the possibilities that lie ahead. Cultivating a positive outlook and practicing gratitude can help us maintain motivation and overcome doubt.

In conclusion, maintaining motivation and momentum is essential to conquering doubt on the path to success. By setting clear goals, surrounding ourselves with positive influences, celebrating achievements, and cultivating a positive mindset, we can push past doubt and continue moving forward. Remember, doubt is just a temporary hurdle, and with determination and perseverance, we can dare to dream and believe to achieve.

Chapter 8: Celebrating Your Achievements

Recognizing and Appreciating Milestones

Milestones are the building blocks of success. They represent significant achievements and serve as markers along the path to reaching our goals. However, in our fast-paced and goal-oriented society, it is easy to overlook these milestones and keep pushing forward without taking the time to recognize and appreciate them. In this subchapter, we will explore the importance of acknowledging and celebrating milestones on our journey to success.

One of the main reasons why recognizing milestones is crucial is that it boosts our confidence and motivation. By acknowledging our progress and giving ourselves credit for the milestones we have achieved, we reinforce our belief in our abilities. This self-assurance helps to combat doubt and instills a sense of determination to keep moving forward. Celebrating milestones also allows us to reflect on the obstacles we have overcome and the growth we have experienced, reminding us that we are capable of conquering doubt.

Another benefit of recognizing milestones is that it provides an opportunity for gratitude. Success is rarely achieved alone, and it is essential to express appreciation for the support and guidance we have received along the way. Whether it's a mentor, a friend, or a family member, acknowledging their contribution not only strengthens our relationships but also reinforces a positive mindset. Gratitude fosters a sense of abundance and attracts more opportunities for growth and success.

Moreover, celebrating milestones allows us to pause and enjoy the journey. It is easy to get caught up in the pursuit of our goals, constantly striving for the next milestone. However, by taking the time to appreciate our achievements, we create moments of joy and fulfillment. These moments serve as reminders of why we started on this path and fuel our passion and determination to continue.

To effectively recognize and appreciate milestones, it is essential to set clear goals and have a system for tracking progress. This can be done through journaling, creating visual representations, or using digital tools. Regularly assessing our progress and celebrating milestones along the way will help to maintain momentum and keep doubt at bay.

In conclusion, recognizing and appreciating milestones is a vital practice on the journey to success. It boosts confidence, cultivates gratitude, and allows us to experience joy along the way. By acknowledging our achievements and expressing appreciation for the support we receive, we reinforce a positive mindset and attract more opportunities for growth. So, let us dare to dream, believe in ourselves, and celebrate each milestone as we conquer doubt on the path to success.

Reflecting on Personal Growth and Development

In the journey of life, personal growth and development are essential elements that shape our paths and determine our success. The subchapter "Reflecting on Personal Growth and Development" in the book "Dare to Dream, Believe to Achieve: Conquering Doubt on the Path to Success" invites all readers, regardless of their background or aspirations, to stop doubting themselves and embrace the transformative power of self-reflection.

Self-reflection is a powerful tool that allows us to take a step back from our busy lives and assess our personal growth journey. It grants us the opportunity to evaluate our strengths, weaknesses, and the progress we have made along the way. By reflecting on our experiences, we gain valuable insights into our own potential and the areas where we may need to invest more time and effort.

One of the first steps in reflecting on personal growth is to acknowledge our doubts. Doubts can hinder our progress and prevent us from reaching our full potential. By addressing and challenging these doubts, we can overcome them and grow stronger. This subchapter provides practical techniques and strategies to help readers recognize and confront their doubts, empowering them to move forward with confidence.

Furthermore, the subchapter emphasizes the importance of setting goals and creating a roadmap for personal development. By defining clear objectives and outlining the necessary steps to achieve them, individuals can measure their progress and stay focused on their journey. It encourages readers to set realistic and achievable goals, both short-term and long-term, and provides guidance on how to stay motivated and overcome obstacles along the way.

Moreover, the subchapter delves into the significance of embracing failure and using it as a stepping stone for growth. It highlights the fact that setbacks are not indicators of failure but rather opportunities for learning and improvement. By reframing failure as a valuable lesson, readers can cultivate a resilient mindset and develop the ability to bounce back stronger than ever.

In conclusion, the subchapter "Reflecting on Personal Growth and Development" is a transformative chapter in the book "Dare to Dream, Believe to Achieve: Conquering Doubt on the Path to Success." It encourages readers from all walks of life to stop doubting themselves and embark on a journey of self-reflection. By recognizing and addressing doubts, setting goals, embracing failure, and consistently evaluating personal growth, readers can discover their true potential and achieve success in all aspects of their lives.

Inspiring Others through Your Success Story

In our journey towards success, we often face moments of doubt and uncertainty. These doubts can be crippling, causing us to question our abilities and hinder our progress. However, it is in these moments that our success stories become even more valuable. By sharing our triumphs and how we overcame doubt, we have the power to inspire others to overcome their own challenges and achieve greatness.

When you share your success story, you provide a beacon of hope for those who may be struggling with doubt. Your story becomes a source of inspiration, reminding others that they too can conquer their fears and achieve their dreams. By sharing your journey, you show others that doubt is merely a temporary obstacle that can be overcome with determination and perseverance.

One of the most powerful aspects of sharing your success story is the connection it creates. Your audience can relate to your struggles, doubts, and fears, making them feel understood and validated. By sharing your personal experiences, you establish a sense of empathy, showing others that they are not alone in their doubts. This connection serves as a catalyst for change, motivating others to push through their doubts and take action towards their goals.

Furthermore, sharing your success story can have a ripple effect. As others witness your achievements and the impact you have made, they may be inspired to pursue their own dreams and aspirations. Your story becomes a catalyst for change, encouraging others to step out of their comfort zones, embrace their passions, and conquer their doubts. By inspiring others through your success, you create a domino effect of empowerment and transformation.

Remember, your success story is not just about you. It is about the countless lives you can touch and inspire. By sharing your journey, you have the power to ignite a fire within others and help them overcome their doubts. So, dare to dream, believe in yourself, and share your success story to inspire others on their own path to success.

Stop doubting yourself and start sharing your success story today. You never know whose life you may change by simply sharing your journey and inspiring others to conquer their doubts. Together, we can create a world where doubt is replaced by unyielding belief, and dreams become a reality.

Chapter 9: Embracing the Journey of Self-Discovery

Exploring Your Passions and Talents

In the journey towards success, doubts often arise and hinder our progress. However, one of the most effective ways to conquer doubt is by exploring our passions and talents. This subchapter aims to guide you in discovering and nurturing your unique abilities, empowering you to overcome any self-doubt while on the path to success.

Passions are the fuel that ignites our inner fire and propels us forward. They are the activities that make us lose track of time, fill us with joy, and give us a sense of purpose. Take a moment to reflect on what truly excites you, what makes you enthusiastic and alive. It could be writing, painting, cooking, playing a musical instrument, or even solving complex mathematical problems. Once you identify your passions, it's essential to find ways to incorporate them into your life. Carve out time each day or week to engage in these activities, as they will not only bring you fulfillment but also help you build confidence in your abilities.

Talents, on the other hand, are the innate gifts and skills that come naturally to us. They are the areas where we excel effortlessly. Identifying your talents can take some introspection and self-awareness. Consider the activities that others often praise you for, the tasks that you find easy to accomplish, or the topics you have an exceptional understanding of. These are potential indicators of your talents. Once you recognize your talents, it is crucial to nurture and develop them further. Seek opportunities to refine your skills, take classes, find mentors, or engage in relevant communities. Cultivating your talents not only boosts your confidence but also opens doors to new opportunities and potential success.

Exploring your passions and talents is a continuous and evolving process. As you delve deeper into your interests, you may discover new passions or talents you were previously unaware of. Embrace this journey of self-discovery with an open mind and a willingness to step outside your comfort zone. Remember, it is through exploring our passions and talents that we learn more about ourselves and gain the confidence needed to conquer doubt.

So, dear reader, take a leap of faith and dare to explore your passions and talents. Believe in yourself and your unique abilities. As you do so, you will find that doubt slowly fades away, replaced by a renewed sense of purpose and a clearer path towards achieving your dreams. Stop doubting and start embracing the power within you.

Embracing Continuous Learning and Personal Growth

In today's rapidly evolving world, where change is constant and success is often determined by one's ability to adapt, embracing continuous learning and personal growth has become more crucial than ever. This subchapter aims to inspire and guide individuals from all walks of life, regardless of their doubts or insecurities, to cultivate a mindset of lifelong learning and personal development.

The path to success is paved with challenges and obstacles that can easily lead to doubt and insecurity. However, by understanding that doubt is a natural part of the journey, individuals can begin to overcome it and embark on a path of personal growth. The first step is to acknowledge that growth is a continuous process and that learning does not end with formal education. By embracing this mindset, individuals can open themselves up to new opportunities and possibilities.

Continuous learning goes beyond acquiring knowledge; it involves actively seeking out new experiences, pushing oneself outside of comfort zones, and being open to feedback and constructive criticism. By doing so, individuals can develop new skills, expand their perspectives, and discover their true potential. This process of personal growth not only enhances one's abilities but also builds confidence and self-belief, enabling individuals to conquer doubt and achieve their dreams.

It is essential to create a conducive environment that fosters continuous learning and personal growth. Surrounding oneself with like-minded individuals, joining professional networks, and seeking mentors or coaches can provide valuable guidance and support. Additionally, developing habits such as reading, attending workshops or seminars, and embracing new technologies can help individuals stay up-to-date with the latest trends and advancements in their respective fields.

Moreover, embracing continuous learning and personal growth requires a growth mindset – the belief that abilities and intelligence can be developed through dedication and hard work. By reframing failures as opportunities for growth and viewing challenges as stepping stones rather than roadblocks, individuals can overcome self-doubt and persevere in their pursuit of success.

In conclusion, embracing continuous learning and personal growth is a fundamental aspect of conquering doubt and achieving success. By adopting a growth mindset, actively seeking new experiences, and surrounding oneself with a supportive community, individuals can break free from the shackles of doubt and unlock their true potential. Remember, the journey of personal growth is ongoing, and every step taken towards learning and self-improvement brings one closer to realizing their dreams.

Living Authentically and Fearlessly

In today's fast-paced and competitive world, it is easy to lose sight of who we truly are and what we want to achieve. Doubt and fear often creep into our minds, preventing us from living authentically and fearlessly. However, it is essential to break free from these barriers if we want to lead a fulfilling and successful life.

Living authentically means being true to ourselves, embracing our uniqueness, and expressing our thoughts, feelings, and beliefs without fear of judgment. It requires us to let go of the need to please others or conform to societal norms. When we live authentically, we are able to tap into our true potential and discover our passions, desires, and purpose in life.

Fear, on the other hand, is a natural human emotion that can either paralyze us or propel us forward. It is often the fear of failure or rejection that holds us back from taking risks and pursuing our dreams. However, living fearlessly does not mean being without fear; it means acknowledging our fears and using them as stepping stones towards personal growth and success.

To live authentically and fearlessly, we must first confront and overcome our doubts. Doubts are the seeds of fear, planted in our minds by our own insecurities and past experiences. By acknowledging these doubts and challenging their validity, we can begin to replace them with self-belief and confidence.

One way to conquer doubt is by setting clear goals and creating a roadmap to achieve them. When we have a clear vision of what we want to accomplish, doubts lose their power over us. Additionally, surrounding ourselves with positive and supportive individuals who believe in our abilities can help us stay motivated and focused on our journey.

Living authentically and fearlessly also requires us to embrace failure as a stepping stone to success. Failure teaches us valuable lessons and helps us grow stronger and wiser. Rather than fearing failure, we should view it as an opportunity for growth and learning.

In conclusion, living authentically and fearlessly is about breaking free from self-doubt and embracing our true selves. It is about setting goals, challenging our doubts, and embracing failure as a part of our journey. By living authentically and fearlessly, we can unlock our full potential and achieve the success and fulfillment we deserve. So, let go of doubt, believe in yourself, and dare to dream big!

Chapter 10: The Power of Belief in Inspiring Others

Sharing Your Journey and Inspiring Change

In life, we often find ourselves doubting our abilities and questioning our path to success. Doubt is a natural part of the human experience, but it doesn't have to define us. In this subchapter, we will explore the power of sharing your journey and how it can inspire change not only in yourself but also in others.

When we share our journey, we create a space for vulnerability and authenticity. It allows us to connect with others on a deeper level, as we realize that we are not alone in our doubts and struggles. By opening up about our own challenges and triumphs, we give others the permission to do the same. This exchange of stories and experiences can be incredibly empowering and liberating.

By sharing your journey, you become a source of inspiration for others. Your story has the potential to touch lives and ignite change in ways you may not even realize. People resonate with authenticity and are drawn to stories of resilience and overcoming obstacles. Your journey can serve as a guiding light for those who are currently doubting themselves, showing them that it is possible to conquer doubt and achieve success.

Furthermore, sharing your journey can create a ripple effect of change. When others witness your transformation and witness the power of perseverance, they may be inspired to embark on their own journey of self-discovery and growth. Your story can serve as a catalyst for change, motivating others to stop doubting and start believing in themselves.

However, it is important to remember that sharing your journey is not about seeking validation or attention. It is about connecting with others and creating a supportive community. It is about using your experiences to uplift and inspire, rather than to boost your ego.

In conclusion, sharing your journey is a powerful tool in conquering doubt and inspiring change. It allows you to connect with others, become a source of inspiration, and create a ripple effect of transformation in the lives of those around you. So, dare to share your story, believe in the impact it can have, and together, let's stop doubting and start believing in our ability to achieve success.

Spreading Positivity and Encouragement

In a world filled with uncertainty and doubt, it is essential to spread positivity and encouragement to overcome the obstacles that hinder our path to success. By cultivating a positive mindset and fostering a supportive environment, we can conquer doubt and achieve our dreams. This subchapter aims to provide insight and strategies to help each and every one of us stop doubting and start believing in ourselves.

Positivity is contagious, and by emanating positive energy, we can uplift not only ourselves but also those around us. It is crucial to surround ourselves with individuals who believe in our potential and offer words of encouragement. By seeking out a support system, we create a network of like-minded individuals who inspire us to push beyond our limits.

One powerful way to spread positivity is through acts of kindness. Small gestures such as offering a helping hand, complimenting others, or expressing gratitude can have a profound impact on our mental well-being. By practicing kindness, we create a ripple effect that extends far beyond our immediate circles, elevating the collective consciousness and creating a more compassionate world.

Another key element in spreading positivity and encouragement is self-belief. Often, doubt arises from within ourselves, fueled by negative self-talk and limiting beliefs. To combat this, we must cultivate a strong belief in our abilities and potential. Affirmations, visualization techniques, and surrounding ourselves with positive affirmations can help reprogram our minds and instill a sense of unwavering self-confidence.

Moreover, embracing failure as a stepping stone to success is crucial. Instead of letting doubt consume us when we stumble, we must view setbacks as valuable lessons and opportunities for growth. By reframing failure as a necessary part of the journey, we can maintain a positive outlook and continue moving forward with renewed determination.

In conclusion, spreading positivity and encouragement is a powerful tool in conquering doubt on the path to success. By cultivating a positive mindset, surrounding ourselves with supportive individuals, practicing kindness, and embracing failure, we can overcome doubt and achieve our dreams. It is through these actions that we create a ripple effect of positivity, inspiring others to stop doubting and start believing in themselves. Dare to dream, believe to achieve – together, we can conquer doubt and unlock our true potential.

Empowering Others to Dare to Dream and Believe to Achieve

Introduction:
In this subchapter, we explore the transformative power of empowering others to dare to dream and believe in their abilities to achieve greatness. Doubt can often hinder our progress and hold us back from reaching our full potential. However, by empowering those around us, we can create a supportive environment that fosters confidence, courage, and a belief in one's own abilities. This subchapter aims to inspire readers to become catalysts for change, encouraging others to overcome doubt and pursue their dreams.

Creating a Supportive Environment:
One of the key aspects of empowering others is to create a supportive environment that nurtures their dreams and aspirations. By offering encouragement, understanding, and a non-judgmental space, we can instill confidence and belief in others. Listening actively, providing constructive feedback, and celebrating their achievements are essential steps towards fostering a positive atmosphere that encourages personal growth.

Leading by Example:
As we embark on our own journey towards conquering doubt and achieving success, it is important to lead by example. Our actions often speak louder than words, and when we display determination, resilience, and a belief in ourselves, we inspire others to do the same. Sharing our own stories of overcoming doubt and achieving success can serve as a source of inspiration, showing others that they too can dare to dream and believe in their abilities.

Encouraging Goal Setting:
Empowering others to dream and achieve requires helping them set meaningful goals. By guiding individuals to define their aspirations, break them down into manageable steps, and create action plans, we enable them to see the path towards their dreams more clearly. Additionally, providing ongoing support

and accountability can help them stay motivated and focused on their goals, even when doubt creeps in.

Building a Supportive Network: Another crucial aspect of empowering others is helping them build a supportive network of like-minded individuals who share their dreams and aspirations. By connecting individuals with mentors, coaches, or peers who have similar goals, we create a community that uplifts and supports each other. This network serves as a valuable resource for advice, motivation, and shared experiences, further fueling their belief in what they can achieve.

Conclusion:
Empowering others to dare to dream and believe in their abilities to achieve is a powerful act that can transform lives. By creating a supportive environment, leading by example, encouraging goal setting, and building a supportive network, we can help others conquer doubt and reach their full potential. Let us become agents of change, inspiring others to stop doubting and start believing in their dreams, for it is in their achievement that the world becomes a better place for all.